What's the Issue?

WHAT'S CYBERBULLYING?

By Emma Jones

KidHaven
PUBLISHING

Published in 2019 by
KidHaven Publishing, an Imprint of Greenhaven Publishing, LLC
353 3rd Avenue
Suite 255
New York, NY 10010

Designer: Andrea Davison-Bartolotta
Editor: Katie Kawa

Photo credits: Cover (top) Peter Dazeley/The Image Bank/Getty Images; cover (bottom) Mikael Damkier/Shutterstock.com; p. 4 Syda Productions/Shutterstock.com; p. 5 (top) HBRH/ Shutterstock.com; p. 5 (bottom) FatCamera/E+/Getty Images; p. 7 (main) Peter Dazeley/ Photographer's Choice/Getty Images; p. 7 (bottom) Rawpixel.com/Shutterstock.com; p. 8 Zivica Kerkez/Shutterstock.com; p. 9 antoniodiaz/Shutterstock.com; p. 11 Uber Images/Shutterstock.com; p. 13 Jeffrey Greenberg/UIG via Getty Images; p. 14 LovArt/Shutterstock.com; p. 15 guteksk7/ Shutterstock.com; p. 17 imtmphoto/Shutterstock.com; p. 18 Lopolo/Shutterstock.com; p. 19 (inset) Owaki/Kulla/Corbis/Shutterstock.com; p. 19 (main) pyzata/Shutterstock.com; p. 20 Pressmaster/ Shutterstock.com; p. 21 Ievgenii Meyer/Shutterstock.com.

Library of Congress Cataloging-in-Publication Data

Names: Jones, Emma, 1983- author.
Title: What's cyberbullying? / Emma Jones.
Description: New York : KidHaven Publishing, [2019] | Series: What's the
 issue? | Includes index.
Identifiers: LCCN 2017061511 (print) | LCCN 2018001190 (ebook) | ISBN
 9781534525948 (eBook) | ISBN 9781534525917 (library bound book) | ISBN
 9781534525924 (pbk. book) | ISBN 9781534525931 (6 pack)
Subjects: LCSH: Cyberbullying–Juvenile literature.
Classification: LCC HV6773.15.C92 (ebook) | LCC HV6773.15.C92 J66 2019
 (print) | DDC 302.34/302854678–dc23
LC record available at https://lccn.loc.gov/2017061511

Printed in the United States of America

CPSIA compliance information: Batch #BS18KL: For further information contact Greenhaven Publishing LLC, New York, New York at 1-844-317-7404.

Please visit our website, www.greenhavenpublishing.com. For a free color catalog of all our high-quality books, call toll free 1-844-317-7404 or fax 1-844-317-7405.

CONTENTS

Two Sides to Technology

Cell phones, computers, tablets, and other **devices** can be used to bring people around the world closer together. They can be used to help people stay in touch no matter how far apart they are. Friends and family members can send each other nice messages and pictures to make each other happy even when they can't see each other.

However, **technology** can also be used to make people feel bad. The use of technology to bully people is called cyberbullying. What can people do to stop cyberbullies? Read on to find out!

Facing the Facts

Around one out of every three children in the United States has been cyberbullied.

Technology can be used to help people, but it can also be used to hurt people. It's up to the person using it to make the right choice.

Different Kinds of Bullying

Cyberbullying is a fairly new problem. It's grown as the use of new technology has grown. However, bullying isn't a new problem. People have been using positions of power to scare or harm others for a long time.

When bullying happens in person, it can include calling people names, pushing or hitting, and making someone feel left out on purpose. Studies have shown that this kind of bullying still happens more often than cyberbullying, but this might change as young people's use of technology changes over time.

Facing the Facts 🔍

The percentage of people who reported being cyberbullied at some point in their life almost doubled between 2007 and 2016.

In many cases, students who are cyberbullied are also bullied while they're at school. Like all kinds of bullying, cyberbullying happens repeatedly, which means it becomes a pattern of hurtful **behavior**.

How Does Cyberbullying Happen?

One reason cyberbullying is such a big problem is because it's hard to get away from it. Today, people are more connected to each other than ever before. There are many different ways people can connect with each other using technology, and cyberbullies can use all of them to hurt others.

Cyberbullies often use smartphones, which allow them to send text messages and emails. Cyberbullies also use social media platforms, which are websites and applications—also known as apps—that allow users to interact with each other and create online communities.

Facing the Facts 🔍

According to a 2015 study, girls are more likely than boys to use social media websites and apps.

8

Some video games allow players to talk to each other and send messages while they play. This can create friendships among players, but it can also lead to cyberbullying.

9

Bullies Without a Name

Cyberbullying often includes posting hurtful **comments** about another person on social media platforms. It can also include calling people hurtful names through text messages or emails. Cyberbullies also use technology to quickly spread **rumors** about other people.

Some websites and apps allow people to post or share things anonymously. This means they can post comments or send messages without using their name. Some people believe this makes bullying easier because people don't have to be **accountable** for their hurtful words. It also makes it harder to find out who bullies are.

Facing the Facts 🔍

More than 80 percent of young people think it's easier to get away with cyberbullying than bullying someone in person.

Some websites or apps don't allow anonymous posting at all. Others allow users to block anonymous messages. This can help fight against cyberbullying because bullies often like to hide who they really are online.

11

Sharing Too Much

Technology can be used to share pictures and other **information** with family and friends. However, people often want to keep some things about themselves private. This can include their full name and address, **embarrassing** pictures and videos, or other personal information. They might not want anyone to see these things, or they might only want to show them to one person or a small group of people.

Cyberbullies sometimes share what's supposed to be private information or pictures through text messages, email, or social media. They often do this to make their **victim** feel embarrassed.

Facing the Facts

Doxing is the act of sharing another person's private information, such as their address and phone number, online without their permission to cause them harm.

Things that are shared on the internet can stay online forever, even if a person thinks they've been deleted. This is why it's important to think carefully about what you share online.

New Problems

Cyberbullying presents many new problems for victims and those who want to help them. One of the biggest problems is the fact that cyberbullies can attack their victims all the time. They don't have to stop bullying when the school day ends or when after-school activities are over. It can be impossible for victims to get away from the bullying.

Cyberbullying is also hard for adults to see unless someone tells them about it. One of the best ways to stop cyberbullying is to tell a trusted adult if you're being bullied or see someone else being bullied online.

Facing the Facts

Many websites and social media platforms have ways to report cyberbullying and block users who are bullies.

Talking to your parents or guardians openly about what you're doing online is a good way to practice internet safety. Also, it's easier to talk about cyberbullying if you're already talking about other online behaviors.

Always ask your parents or guardians before

sharing personal information online

meeting someone you've only talked to online

posting pictures online

using a social media platform for the first time

downloading apps, games, pictures, videos, or songs

The Effects of Cyberbullying

In some cases, adults might begin to realize a child is being cyberbullied when they see changes in the child's behavior. Cyberbullying can **affect** young people in many different ways. Victims of cyberbullying often feel alone, and they start to see themselves in a negative, or bad, way. This is also known as having poor self-esteem.

Cyberbullying can also cause victims to lose interest in school, spending time with friends, or activities they once liked. They might feel scared, too, because they can't get away from the bullying.

Facing the Facts 🔍

According to a 2017 study, 41 percent of adults in the United States have been victims of cyberbullying.

Cyberbullying can make victims feel alone, afraid, and angry. Talking to a trusted adult can help a victim deal with what they're going through in a healthy way.

Getting Help

If a victim of cyberbullying tells someone what they're going through, they can often get the help they need. Adults can help victims of cyberbullying take screenshots, or pictures, of harmful messages or posts. Screenshots can be used to prove that someone is being cyberbullied.

Schools often have plans in place to deal with all kinds of bullying, including cyberbullying. If a cyberbully is telling their victim they are going to hurt them, it should be reported to the police. All 50 states have laws in place that deal with bullying.

Facing the Facts 🔍

The U.S. government first began collecting information about bullying in schools in 2005.

School officials and the police are trained to handle different kinds of bullying. If cyberbullies also bully their victims at school, school officials should be told. If cyberbullies say they're going to act **violently**, the police should take action.

Dealing with the Problem

If you or someone you know is being cyberbullied, you don't have to feel helpless. There are many things you can do to get help and make the bullying stop, but the first thing you should do is tell an adult. No one should have to deal with bullying on their own.

Cyberbullying affects kids and adults around the world. It's important to talk openly about it so leaders and other adults can learn more about the problem. This can help them come up with plans to stop cyberbullying and make everyone feel safe online.

20

Facing the Facts 🔍

Students who are bullied find the actions of other students to be more helpful than adults' actions, according to a 2010 study.

WHAT CAN YOU DO?

Talk to your parents or guardians about your online activity.

Don't share rumors or other hurtful posts online.

Don't share your passwords with anyone.

Tell an adult if you're being cyberbullied or if you see cyberbullying happening.

If you know someone who's being cyberbullied, be nice to them. Remind them they're not alone.

Be kind and respectful to others online and in person.

Start or be part of a group at school that stands against bullying.

These are just some of the ways you can keep yourself safe online and help others who are being cyberbullied. Do you know any other

GLOSSARY

accountable: Required to explain actions or choices.

affect: To produce an effect on something.

behavior: The way a person acts.

comment: A statement of opinion about something.

device: A tool used for a certain purpose.

embarrassing: Causing a feeling of foolishness.

information: Knowledge or facts about something.

rumor: A story passed from one person to another that has not been proven to be true.

technology: The method of using science to solve problems. Also, the tools used to solve those problems.

victim: A person who is hurt by someone else.

violent: Relating to the use of bodily force to hurt others.

FOR MORE INFORMATION

WEBSITES

Kids Against Bullying

pacerkidsagainstbullying.org

This website provides information on dealing with all kinds of bullying, including cyberbullying.

StopBullying.gov: What Kids Can Do

www.stopbullying.gov/kids/what-you-can-do/index.html

This U.S. government website offers tips on what to do if you or someone you know is being bullied.

BOOKS

Gifford, Clive. *Super Social Media and Awesome Online Safety*. New York, NY: Crabtree Publishing Company, 2018.

Lindeen, Mary. *Digital Safety Smarts: Preventing Cyberbullying*. Minneapolis, MN: Lerner Publishing Group, 2016.

Yearling, Tricia. *How Do I Stay Safe from Cyberbullies?* New York, NY: Enslow Publishing, 2016.

INDEX